GU00731386

# DISCERNING AND PREPARING FOR RELIGIOUS LIFE

## A guide for women

by
Rachael Marie Collins

*All booklets are published thanks to the
generous support of the members of the
Catholic Truth Society*

CATHOLIC TRUTH SOCIETY
PUBLISHERS TO THE HOLY SEE

# Content

*This booklet is an abridged version of a book "Called by God",
published by Roman Catholic Books (2017). All rights reserved. First
published 2016 by the Incorporated Catholic Truth Society, 40-46
Harleyford Road London SE11 5AY Tel: 020 7640 0042 Fax: 020
7640 0046. © 2016 The Incorporated Catholic Truth Society.*

*ISBN 978 1 78469 135 6*

*And just so, he has called women in all times to the most intimate union with him: they are to be emissaries of his love, proclaimers of his will to kings and popes, and forerunners of his Kingdom in the hearts of men.* To be the Spouse of Christ *is the most sublime vocation which has been given, and whosoever sees this way open before her will yearn for no other way.*

St Edith Stein

# INTRODUCTION

*Easter Week 2015*
*Year of Consecrated Life*

Dear Marie Therese,

There is a dearth of materials for those discerning or preparing for entry into religious life. Much is available to assist couples preparing for marriage, but very little specifically tailored for those called to religious life.

It must seem presumptuous for me as a married woman to write about discernment and preparation for religious life. I do not know religious life but I do know what it is to discern (having done so at your age) and I do know what it is to be (and remain!) a beginner in the spiritual life.

This book is for young women like you, who are just starting the discernment process. It is based on my own discernment, which started at fourteen and continued, on and off, until I was twenty-three. More importantly, it draws on the wisdom of our saintly sisters in Christ - women who understood and embodied what St John Paul II called our "feminine genius" (*Mulieris Dignitatem*) - St Teresa of Avila, St Thérèse of Lisieux, St Zélie Martin, St Faustina, St Teresa of the Andes, and Blessed Elizabeth of the Trinity, to name but a few.

My aim is to provide you with an overview of the spiritual life and discernment process, and to guide you to richer, more formidable authors and resources that you can delve into as needed. Some of these authors are modern; many are from our past. All contribute to the rich spiritual tradition of the Church.

You might find some of these things difficult and challenging. Christ does challenge us, yes. But he also invites us - in whatever state of life he intends for us - to joyful union with him; *he makes possible* a life richer and more fulfilling than any we can imagine for ourselves.

Older religious might be reminded of their own formation. Why, they might ask, would these younger generations embrace a spirituality that is so exacting? Because nothing less than a full gift of self - whether that be in marriage or religious life - will satisfy! Nothing less than an offering of our all - even though we know that in trying for the ideal of Christ, we will inevitably fail - will quench the desires of our heart (*Ps* 37:3-7).

Fortunately, Christ meets us in our failures and it is only when we offer all of ourselves to him - the broken bits as well as the whole bits - the failures as well as our successes - that he can transform us into our true selves: radiant daughters of God. It is a rigorous way of life but with humility, perseverance and grace, you will find it joyful and beautiful.

I hope this book is helpful to you. I also hope it will assist fathers, mothers, siblings and priests in supporting their daughters, sisters and parishioners as they progress towards union with Christ.

Love,

Rachael Marie

# DISCERNMENT AS COURTSHIP

Dear Marie Therese,

It can take a long time to discern a call to religious life. Don't be disheartened that you still aren't sure what God is asking of you.

Part of the problem is that you haven't been told how to discern. It is difficult to accomplish something when you don't know where to start or how to proceed.

Some souls know from a very early age that they are called to belong to him and to him alone.[1] St Faustina knew at age seven and first sought entry into the religious life at eighteen. St Thérèse of Lisieux, your namesake, also knew from an early age and first tried to enter Carmel at age fourteen.

It is more common to spend many years in discernment.[2] It took St Thérèse's parents many years to discern that they were *not* called to religious life. Saints Zélie and Louis Martin were told at ages twenty and twenty-two respectively that they did not have a vocation to religious life, despite yearning for such a life for many years. Louis remained single for nearly fifteen years before marrying Zélie in 1858 aged thirty-five. Zélie was twenty-nine.

It is frustrating that you cannot clearly see what path you are called to take. This can lead to impatience or a sense of having been abandoned. This cross of unknowing, however, can be a great gift.

This time of discernment is really a period of preparation and training - preparation for and training in the religious life. For this is how one discerns.

It is also a period of courtship. Throughout this stage of discernment, Jesus desires you for himself and wants you to learn how to love him more perfectly.

During a Christian courtship, people discern whether they should marry. They learn about one another. They develop ways and patterns of speaking with and relating to one another. They also help one another with acts of love and service. As they discern together, they slowly and prudently start to lay a foundation for marriage.

Your courtship with Christ is no different. Get to know him. Spend regular time with him in prayer. Develop a way of relating to him and being preesnt to him. Allow him into your heart. Allow him to court you and love you.

In the same way that a woman will allow her fiancé to lift something heavy for her or perhaps help her father with a repair around the house or some other manly work, allow Jesus as your betrothed or possible future spouse to do much for you. You do not have to do the heavy lifting by yourself anymore. He is waiting for your permission to help you.

Jesus will shower your soul with many graces during this period of discernment, if you are willing to receive them. Your discernment period is a time to draw closer to God. It is a time to develop a rich interior life so that you: (a) are ready to enter religious life if called; or (b) can continue with life in the world in a solid and holy way should it be God's will that you serve him as a lay person.

The desire to give oneself entirely to Christ is a grace from Jesus. Even if you are not called to religious life, it pleases him that you are sincere in seeking out his will for you and trying to conform to it.

Ask Jesus to give you the grace to endure this wait patiently. In moments of difficulty or impatience, meditate on Christ's hidden life - the life he led from birth to age thirty.[3]

For thirty years he knew who he was and what he was to do for us, and yet he waited all that time. He spent this time honouring, loving and assisting his mother, Mary, and his adoptive father St Joseph, praying, practising his carpentry trade and diligently fulfilling all his duties of state.[4]

Here you have the perfect model to follow. Ask Jesus of the Hidden Life to help you use this time of discernment and preparation well. Try to be productive and intentional in how you live during this wait. It is given to you to prepare: pray, read and study, attend Holy Mass, work and grow in a life of regular prayer and the sacraments.

Like Christ, live frugally. Like Christ, behave, dress and speak modestly. Like Christ, support your family. Like Christ, fulfil all your duties of state. Like Christ, devote yourself to prayer and the diligent study of Sacred Scripture and the Catholic faith. Like Christ, engage in disciplined work.

The discernment period will also be used by Our Lord to reveal areas in which you need to grow. Some souls might need to overcome the faults of impatience and self-absorption. Others might need to grow in forbearance, fidelity or courage.

St Faustina allowed her parents' opposition to deter her from entering the convent. "Interiorly", she "shunned God" and "tried...to stifle it [the incessant call of grace] with amusements". Jesus rebuked her in a vision. He said to her, "How long shall I put up with you and how long will you keep putting me off?"[5]

Faustina begged Jesus for the grace to know what to do. When he revealed what this was, she took decisive and immediate action. She left home, and travelled immediately to Warsaw as instructed by Our Lord. Jesus gave her the grace to overcome her timidity.

St Faustina's response illustrates how we should approach obstacles, trials or weaknesses uncovered during the discernment period. Take the matter to Jesus and Mary, and ask for their assistance.

Beg God for the graces you need to overcome any faults he reveals to you during this period of courtship. Specifically request the graces of perseverance, patience, purity, humility, courage, fidelity and wisdom. Ask Our Lady to intercede on your behalf. Visit him often in the Blessed Sacrament and ask him for the assistance you need.

# PREPARATION AS DISCERNMENT

Dear Marie Therese,

The best way to discern whether you are called to religious life is to *prepare* for religious life.

When St Thomas More discerned whether he should become a priest, he did so by engaging in "exercises of piety, looking to and pondering on the priesthood in vigils, fasts and prayers and similar austerities."[6] In other words, his discernment was a form of preparation - he entered deeply into the spiritual life and, in doing so, obtained an answer as to his vocation. His biographer notes that the saint was more thoroughly prepared for the priesthood than most candidates who do enter.

Follow the example of St Thomas More. If you feel an attraction for the religious life or wonder whether it might be for you, then prepare for it. Act as if you are called. Say a prayer of obstruction[7] and take all the necessary steps to enter. This is how you discern.[8]

Approaching discernment in this way will help you remain peaceful and detached. Discernment is aptly described as an *agony* and it is easy to become angst-ridden.[9] Try to be detached about your need for certainty. When you ask God for light regarding your vocation, he hears you and he will respond. Perhaps not when you want him to respond, but he will do so in his time. He *will* guide you in this.

Pray to God for the strength, wisdom and generosity to get on with the task of preparing for and entering religious life. And then start. There is nothing more important than this.

# A SUPERNATURAL VOCATION

Dear Marie Therese,

One of the reasons it took me so long to discern my vocation was that I was constantly looking for absolute certainty about whether or not I was called. I was told to consider whether I was "called" but I wasn't sure what that "calling" looked or felt like. I was told to seek out the deepest desires of my heart - that my true vocation would satisfy me in a way that the other options would not. But I wasn't sure how to identify the deepest desires of my heart.

While I really did desire to enter religious life, the methodology I used to discern was seriously flawed. It is unfortunate that the modern approach to discernment encourages young women to focus on their subjective and inconsistent feelings and desires. This is not advisable.

First, our emotions and desires - especially those that are unexamined or superficial - tend to be changeable. They are affected by our imagination and moods. An unpurified, immature imagination, for example, can distort our ability to see things (including ourselves) accurately. This is why it is so important to monitor our intake of media - especially magazines, pop music and television programmes - which can influence the way we feel, imagine or think about important things such as love, marriage, sex and God.[10]

Second, marriage is a *natural* vocation while religious life is a *supernatural* vocation. What I mean by this is that our *natural* inclination is to want marriage. We almost all desire the companionship and joy a spouse and children can bring. Because it is necessary for a properly ordered civil society, marriage has had a long and widespread existence. Marriage existed before Christ was born; it continues to exist in both ancient and neo-pagan cultures now.

In other words, marriage doesn't depend on faith in God or a particular, special calling from God in the way that a religious vocation does. Yes, Christ did make marriage a sacrament. It is a beautiful means of obtaining sanctity but this does not change the fact that marriage is also the *natural default* to which we all gravitate. It is simply part of how we are built.

The religious life is *naturally* less attractive because it involves a radical death to self from the very beginning. Marriage also involves a great death to self - it just happens more slowly and is less obvious at the start. Having a spouse and raising children is hard work. To do it well means much sacrifice and constant self-denial for the sake of others. Even in marriage, one must endure suffering: you cannot avoid the cross.

One important consequence of all this is that you can and sometimes should choose against the natural inclination to marriage. In other words, a desire for and attraction to marriage doesn't rule out that one is also called to religious life.

Don't give any significance to superficial feelings or desires. When you do examine your feelings and emotions, focus on these two things: (a) your conscience, and (b) which option gives you the greatest sense of peace - not excitement, passion or short-lived certainty, but peace.

Read *The Discernment of Spirits* by Father Timothy Gallagher OMV for further instruction and guidance on this part of your discernment process.

Reading List

Timothy Gallagher OMV, *The Discernment of Spirits*

Francis de Sales, *Finding God's Will for You*

# A Superior Way of Life

**D**ear Marie Therese,

    Religious vocations should be a "normal thing in Christian life".[11] The sentiment that they are rare and unusual is at odds with scripture, the writings of the saints, and the counsel of St Thomas Aquinas.

In *1 Corinthians* 7, St Paul exhorts those who can enter into religious life to do so. It is, he says, the better way of life:

> …he who marries his betrothed does well; and he who refrains from marriage will do better.

St Paul is right. Objectively, it is the more perfect way of life. It enables the soul to embrace God without the distractions of having to provide and care for a spouse and child. Under such conditions, the soul can progress more rapidly in the spiritual life:[12]

> The unmarried man is anxious about the affairs of the Lord, how to please the Lord; but the married man is anxious about worldly affairs, how to please his wife.

And his interests are divided. And the unmarried woman or girl is anxious about the affairs of the Lord, how to be holy in body and spirit; but the married woman is anxious about worldly affairs, how to please her husband.

Like St Paul, St Thomas Aquinas also considered religious life to be a "greater good". He describes the religious state as a "spiritual schooling for the attainment of the perfection of charity"[13] and states that:[14]

…it is certain that entrance into religion [religious life] is a greater good, and to doubt about this is to disparage Christ who gave this counsel.

The Angelic Doctor warns that those who fail to see religious life as an objectively superior good, "disparage Christ". This is because the evangelical counsels (also known as the counsels of perfection: poverty, chastity and obedience) were given to us by Christ and those who choose to live by them (as nuns and religious sisters do) go beyond what is merely necessary for salvation and opt for the way of perfection.

Christ introduces us to the evangelical counsels in *Matthew 19*. Here Jesus raises the idea of celibacy, telling us that "there are eunuchs who have made themselves eunuchs for the sake of the kingdom of heaven" and that "[h]e who is able to receive this, let him receive it" (*Mt* 19:12). Those who choose virginity for love of God, he says, are "like angels in heaven" (*Mt* 22:30).

Later we are told of the rich young man who asks Jesus what he must do to have eternal life (*Mt* 19:16-30).[15] Our Lord starts by telling the young man to obey the commandments (*Mt* 19:16-19):

> And behold, one came up to him, saying "Teacher, what good deed must I do, to have eternal life?" And he said to him, "Why do you ask me about what is good? One there is who is good. If you would enter life, keep the commandments." He said to him, "Which?" And Jesus said, "You shall not kill, You shall not commit adultery, You shall not steal, You shall not bear false witness, Honour your father and mother, and, You shall love your neighbour as yourself."

When the young man responds that he does all this, Our Lord invites him to abandon everything and to follow him (*Mt* 19:20-21):

> The young man said to him, "All these I have observed; what do I still lack?" Jesus said to him, "If you would be perfect, go, sell what you possess and give to the poor, and you will have treasure in heaven; and come, follow me."

Our Lord invites the young man into a life of poverty and obedience: He invites the young man to enter religious life.

Sadly, many religious are uncomfortable with this teaching. They are reluctant to see their celibate life of poverty and obedience as objectively superior in any way.

They are afraid to tell my generation and now yours what the Church has always taught: religious life is the more perfect path to take if one desires to be a saint.

Keep in mind that this teaching does not denigrate marriage.[16] I don't doubt that I can become a saint through marriage, and I am extremely grateful to God for my marriage, my husband and our children.[17] However, it is also true that while marriage is good and beautiful, spiritually speaking, the religious life is outstanding.

The Second Vatican Council addressed this issue in *Optatam Totius*, wherein Pope Paul VI instructed seminarians to "recognise the *surpassing excellence*[18] of virginity consecrated to Christ so that with a maturely deliberate and generous choice they may consecrate themselves to the Lord by a complete gift of body and soul."[19]

This doctrine of the Church was again reiterated by St John Paul II in his 1996 Apostolic Exhortation, *Vita Consecrata*:[20]

As a way of showing forth the Church's holiness, *it is to be recognised that the consecrated life*, which mirrors Christ's own way of life, *has an objective superiority*. …The consecrated life proclaims and in a certain way anticipates the future age, when the fullness of the Kingdom of heaven, already present in its first fruits and in mystery, will be achieved, and when the children of the resurrection will take neither wife nor husband, but will be like the angels of God (cf. *Mt* 22:30).

It is important to note here that St John Paul II describes the consecrated life as "objectively" superior. This objectivity relates to the general efficacy of this way of life in attaining holiness (all things being equal) rather than its suitability for a particular person. Subjectively, a person should do what God wants her to do. Nevertheless, where there is a choice - that is, if a person can live the religious life because they have the aptitude for it and are called - they *should* choose it since it provides a better means for achieving sanctity.

Even non-Catholics can understand this. In her book, *Three Came Home*, Agnes Newton Keith writes about her experience in a Japanese prisoner-of-war camp during World War II where she was interned for a number of years with a large group of Catholic nuns and religious sisters. "I was thrown in close contact with a community of Roman Catholic nuns", and this was, she says, "[t]he best thing that happened to me in captivity."[21] Prior to this, the non-Catholic Agnes "really knew nothing about them":[22]

> Now in Kuching, I met nuns, as women, and sisters, and mothers; hard workers, and my friends. Here I met them as people who sang, and laughed, and made jokes and had fun. As people who prayed and fasted as a privilege and a joy, not as a duty. As women who had chosen a way of life, not had it thrust on them, and who loved it. As women who were sorry for *us*, merciful to *us*, tried to help *us*, because *they* had the Way and the Life; while we,

poor fleshly creatures of this world and now cut off from this world, had nothing.

We secular women, living with our own sex had already found ourselves, and found ourselves wanting. ...But the sisters were different, they were complete. They were wedded to Christ and the Church, and for the first time in my life in Kuching, I saw that this was so. Then for the first time it became credible to me that they were Holy Brides.

Agnes was so impressed with the sisters that she sought to understand what made them so different to the other women in the camp:[23]

All through camp life, I studied the sisters and loved them, and I tried very hard to learn. I learned one thing: ...We wives had put our minds and our hearts on our husbands, which is what a good marriage is, and we now were without them, and lost. The sisters had put minds and hearts on God only, and they had Him, and they only were whole.

The calling to religious life is a great gift. It isn't given to everyone and those who do receive it should be grateful. If Our Lord asks you to follow him in ascending the path of perfection, are you ready to say yes or, like the rich young man, will you turn away?

Reading List

The Evangelical Counsels

*Poverty*

Thomas Dubay SM, *Happy Are You Poor: The Simple Life and Spiritual Freedom*

*Celibacy*

Thomas Dubay SM, *"And You Are Christ's": The Charism of Virginity and the Celibate Life*

Andrew Apostoli CFR, *When God Asks for an Undivided Heart: Choosing Celibacy in Love and Freedom*

*Obedience*

Reginald Garrigou-Lagrange OP, *The Three Ages of the Interior Life: Prelude to Eternal Life*, Volume 2, Part 3, Chapter 15: "The Grandeur of Obedience".

# VOCARE:
## "TO CALL" AND "TO NAME"

Dear Marie Therese,

Your efforts to discern will likely be hindered rather than helped by the general confusion surrounding the word "vocation". St Teresa Benedicta of the Cross, better known as Edith Stein, wrote about this problem in 1931:[24]

> In everyday usage, the hackneyed word "vocation" retains little of its original connotation. When young people are about to graduate, one wonders what occupation they should pursue; the question whether women should enter professional life or stay at home has been controversial for some time. Here the term designating vocation does not convey much more than gainful employment. The original meaning of the word survives only in particular allusions, i.e. when one says that a person has missed his vocation or when one speaks of a religious vocation. These idioms signify that a vocation is something to which a person must be *called*.

Even then, "vocation" had become synonymous with "occupation"; a conflation which obscures the true and original meaning of the word. This confusion is the reason one sometimes hears people speaking about their professional life in vocational terms. It is also why many young people decide on an occupation, industry or field of work before considering whether they might be called to the priesthood or religious life.

"Vocation" is derived from the Latin word, "*vocare*" meaning to "call". In Italian, it also means to "name". St Edith Stein asked, "Yet, what does it mean to be called?" Her answer was that a "call must have been sent from someone, to someone, *for something* in a *distinct manner*."[25] Vocation, as such, is relational. It is about one's intimate relationship with God and what God intends for us through this relationship.

He is calling us, first and foremost, to be his daughters and sons. He is calling us into a relationship with him in which he "names" us as his own: "I have called you by name" (*Is* 43:1). This is the universal call to sanctity.

Second, he calls us further into a familial relationship with him through which we mirror him in a particular and irreplaceable way. God invites some women to enter the religious life: he asks them to unite themselves exclusively and entirely to him. In this they mirror Christ. They become living icons of the Son (Second Person of the Holy Trinity) in his relationship to the Father (First Person of the Holy Trinity) and the way that the Son generously sacrificed himself on earth - on the cross - out of love for the Father, for all of the Father's children. It is a love that is directed towards the One but flows out to all.

Others are to be wives and mothers: they become co-operators with his creative power as mothers and co-workers in his redemptive effort as they work and pray for the salvation and well-being of their husbands and children. It is in the specificity of her vocational love that the wife and mother becomes a living icon of the Holy Spirit (the Third Person of the Holy Trinity). The Holy Spirit is the love of the Father (the First Person) for the Son (the Second Person) and vice versa: He is the Love of a specific Person for a specific Person. The wife and mother is asked to direct herself towards the One in a love that flows out to affect (primarily) a specific one or few (her husband and any children they have).

When one enters into religious life or marriage, a gift is given and that gift is a "person". When I married I was given the gift of my husband. He gave himself to me and I to him. A religious sister is given the gift of a person too: the gift of Christ himself as her spouse. He gives himself to her and she gives herself to him. This relational aspect is what makes these "vocations" so significant and beautiful. A person is of infinite worth. One's spouse (earthly or heavenly) is irreplaceable. One's children are irreplaceable.

When I left my job as an attorney, my work, office and desk were allocated to another attorney. My work (the tertiary sense of "vocation"; better known as "avocation") was replicable. This is not so as a wife and mother. The person-to-person relationships and interactions between my family members and me are unique.

The emphasis placed in these states of life (marriage and religious life) on relationships - particularly one's intimate relationship with God - orientates the woman toward eternity. The relationship she enters into with God and then the souls she encounters and loves in his name extends beyond time and place. This distinguishes religious life and marriage from avocational work. I will not take the legal papers I wrote as an attorney with me to heaven but I do hope to share the beatific vision with my husband and children. Likewise, the religious sister aspires to enter into eternity where she can forever praise and behold her Eternal Spouse.

Because the religious life is a supernatural calling - it is something above and beyond what we are naturally inclined to - it stands out as a very particular and special calling. Some people fall into marriage by default. They do not enter into the married state with the conscious purpose of serving and loving God. It is very difficult to "fall" into religious life - one chooses religious life because one makes a conscious choice in favour of God and heaven.

Given the hierarchy of the different senses of the word "vocation", it is appropriate to determine who you are called to be and what you intend to do in a similarly hierarchical manner. When you consider whether you are called to religious life, try to answer these questions in the following order:

1. Do I want to be a saint?

2. If yes, am I called to be a nun or religious sister?

3. If yes, does God want me in a contemplative or semi-active order? Which order should I join?

4. If no (I am not called to religious life), should I enter into the married state? If yes, to whom?

5. If I am to marry or remain celibate in the world, what occupation or gainful employment should I pursue?

Ask St Edith Stein to aid you in these deliberations. She understands discernment and she will intercede on your behalf to obtain the clarity you need.

# Stages of Formation:
## Room for Error

Dear Marie Therese,

The discernment process does not end when you enter the convent but continues as you progress through the various stages of formation. Unlike marriage, which by its nature must be permanent and exclusive from the very start, religious life does not ripen into permanency until solemn vows have been professed.

There are a number of stages you must pass through first - all of which are designed to help you and your religious community see whether you really do have a vocation to religious life. This is a process of "dual discernment" whereby you continue to discern if you have a vocation to religious life and the religious community continues to discern if you have a vocation with them.

The first stage is the postulancy. You'll have somewhere between four and twenty-four months as a postulant (depending on the order and whether it is semi-active or contemplative). Next you'll enter the novitiate phase. You'll be a novice for another year or two. Following this is the first profession where you'll make temporary vows in which you commit to living as a religious sister for another two to three years. In some orders you'll then renew these temporary vows for another two years. Only after all this, do you make a profession of perpetual vows. You will have "tried" the religious life for at least six years before making a permanent commitment - often longer.

In *The Song at the Scaffold*, Gertrud von Le Fort likens the novitiate to "a question which can be answered in the negative."[26] At some point along the way, you might be told that it is not for you. You might not be accepted by the order of your choice. Conversely, you might realise that this is not where God wants you. You can leave any time during the postulancy or novitiate, which means, of course, that you can "try" religious life without permanently closing the door to marriage.

If you question whether you are called then enter. Entrust the process to God. Say a prayer of obstruction asking God to keep you from entering religious life if this is not his will for you. Then proceed prayerfully and courageously.

Reading List

Pierre de Calan, *Cosmas or the Love of God* (fiction)

Gertrud von Le Fort, *The Song at the Scaffold* (fiction)

Rumer Godden, *In This House of Brede* (fiction)

# A UNIVERSAL CALL TO SANCTITY

**D**ear Marie Therese,

Marriage and religious life require similar preparation in so far as the call to be a saint is universal, and the way we become saints is the same for everyone: seeking union with God by living out God's will, with him, every moment of every day. The basic tools for achieving this are the same regardless of one's state of life, for sanctity cannot be achieved without a rich prayer life, the sacraments and a disavowal and avoidance of sin. Detachment, self-denial and prayer is asked of all.

Of course, certain aspects of one's preparation will differ according to the state of life one is preparing for. How the universal call to sanctity is lived out on a day-to-day basis varies and, therefore, some of the practical means of preparation will also vary.

An enclosed nun pours herself out in prayer and obedience. She serves Our Lord and his Church through her primary "work" of prayer. One enclosed contemplative I know has adopted my home country as a special apostolate of hers. Although she has never been to Australia, she offers her routine and day of prayer, her obedience and her struggles, joys and suffering at least in part for the Catholic Church and its members in Australia. Hers is an interior service. She is an apostle of prayer.

A sister in a semi-active order also prays, and this is (or rather should be) the foundation of all she does. In addition to this, however, she is also called to participate in active service.[27] A Sister of Life might run a healing retreat for post-abortive women, or she might spend time praying with a young woman discerning whether to place her baby for adoption. A Franciscan Sister of the Renewal (colloquially known as the CFR sisters) might spend part of her day running a soup kitchen or teaching catechesis to children at a parish in a poor neighbourhood. A Dominican Sister might also be a kindergarten or high school teacher.

Similarly, a woman who marries should pour herself out in prayer and service. Like a semi-active sister, the life of a married woman must be rooted in prayer and service but the form of her service is somewhat narrower and more focused than that of a religious sister. A sister might serve the people in one community and then, when transferred to a different convent of the same order, she will work with yet another group of people in a different area with different needs. In contrast, the primary recipients of a mother's service are unchanging. The service of a wife and mother must be constantly directed towards the good of her spouse and any children given to the marriage.

# SPIRITUAL DIRECTION

Dear Marie Therese,

When we first spoke of your desire to enter religious life, I told you how important it is to find a good confessor and spiritual director. This is especially vital given the doubts and confusion you have sometimes experienced over the matter of your vocation.

Generally Jesus will direct a soul through the intermediary of a priestly spiritual director. Jesus remains the true director of every soul, but asks us to use the means he has provided. He has given us the Sacrament of Confession for this end. In confession we reveal our souls in such an intimate way that it is possible for Jesus (through his priest) to give us spiritual direction *par excellence*.

In some Catholic movements it has become popular to have a layperson act as one's spiritual director. I pass no judgment on this for the laity. However, anyone discerning religious life should have a priest as a spiritual director. The priest has the grace of state and stands in for Christ in a special way.[28]

Find a good and holy priest to hear your confessions - preferably on a weekly basis - and to direct you in the spiritual life. If there is no such priest available to you, beg God to send you one.

The priest should be humble and faithful. Look for a priest with self-restraint. It is beneficial for him to have had some experience directing souls either living the religious life or preparing for entry into religious life. Both St Teresa of Avila and St Francis de Sales list prudence as being a particularly important trait in a director. Avoid directors who are rash or impulsive.[29]

The direction of a competent confessor can facilitate great progress in the spiritual life. He will help you avoid mistakes, see faults that need correcting, and hold you back from excess[30] and scruples.[31]

A good confessor will also help you discern whether you have a calling or not. Often - as was the case for me - your confessor will see before you do whether or not you have a religious vocation.

When you do find a competent spiritual director, read the advice contained in St Francis de Sales' superb treatise, *An Introduction to the Devout Life*.[32] St Francis advises us to be candid, sincere and frank in how we speak to our director:

> Let him know the good and the bad that you are in, without lying or dissimulation. In acting thus, the good in you will be assessed and confirmed, and the bad will be corrected and remedied. Your pains will be alleviated and your joys moderated.[33]

Do not fret. Entrust this need to Jesus.

Reading List

Francis de Sales, *Introduction to the Devout Life*:
Part I, Chapter 4 ("The Pursuit of the Devout Life Requires
a Guide") and Part II, Chapter 19 ("Of Holy Confession")

Reginald Garrigou-Lagrange OP, *The Three Ages of the
Interior Life: Prelude of the Eternal Life*, Volume 1, Part 1,
Chapter 17: "Spiritual Direction"

Brett A. Brannen, *To Save a Thousand Souls*, Chapter 7
("The Importance of a Spiritual Director")

# THE SPIRITUAL LIFE

Dear Marie Therese,

I have spoken much of the "spiritual life" but have not yet defined or clarified what I mean by this.

The spiritual life is your soul's intimacy with Jesus. It is your growth in and towards God. It is the action of his grace in your soul and it is the progress made by your soul as Christ brings it into an intimate union with him. It cannot be had without prayer and the sacraments.

Prayer is the work of the spiritual life. St Thérèse of Lisieux tells us that "prayer is an aspiration of the heart, it is a simple glance directed to heaven, it is a cry of gratitude and love in the midst of trial as well as joy; finally it is something great, supernatural, which expands my soul and unites me to Jesus."[34]

The terms, "prayer" and "spiritual life", refer to subtly different things but they are inclusive of one another and mutually dependent. Where you are in your spiritual life will impact your prayer. Correspondingly, one is dependent upon prayer to maintain and advance in one's spiritual union with God.

As a religious, the spiritual life will be your true "work". This is true of those called to the semi-active life as well as those who enter a contemplative order. Your life of prayer and your sacramental life should be the foundation of all you do. As a religious, all your other work should flow from and be strengthened by this primary "work".

This also applies to the laity. Right now you are in the lay world living a lay pre-vocation. Now is the time for you to develop your spiritual life. Make prayer, receiving the sacraments and a life of mortification your primary "work" from which all your other activities flow.

As a single woman in good physical health and of sound mind, there is no impediment to your preparing for religious life in this way. In fact, your entry into this way of life will assist you and your director in determining whether you are called to religious life.

St Teresa of Avila writes much on the stages of prayer and the spiritual life. Read her autobiography, *Life*. This will help you understand the different types of prayer - the path of prayer through which God will lead you - as well as the various stages of the spiritual life.

I can provide a rough summary of some things you can expect.

Be prepared at the beginning for two things: First, that prayer will often feel like hard work. You will find at the start - and recurring throughout other stages of the spiritual life - that you will do a lot of the talking. You'll find yourself having to do a lot of one-way conversation with God, reading spiritual books and reciting vocal prayers.

Establish fixed times for prayer, and a daily routine. Stick to this routine. It will seem like a lot of work but God hears you and your effort pleases him. Slowly and surely - if done with an earnest and humble spirit - you will make progress.

Second, at the start, you will be granted many sweet consolations. These are like the little treats I give to the children from time to time to encourage good behaviour, and to show my love and affection for them. In these moments, you will feel great joy and lightness. To begin with, these consolations will be emotional in nature or consist of an intellectual light. That is, they usually invoke the emotions or intellect.

These consolations are unmerited gifts from God, given as a sign of love and encouragement as he sees fit. Be careful not to seek them out. They cannot be earned. Ask for a spirit of gratitude rather than one of entitlement.

Moving forward you will also experience periods of dryness and darkness.

These stages are meant to purify you. There is only so much we can do to purify ourselves. Only God himself can perfect our souls and he does so - in part - by introducing darkness and dryness into our spiritual life and our work of prayer.

Early on it will be limited to the absence of emotional consolations. There will be no sweetness offered by God and your prayer will feel like hard work. When this occurs, practise mental prayer as before, and continue with your regular prayer routine.

This period does not last forever but it helps strengthen you. This is one way Our Lord corrects your motives. You begin to pray and lead a sacramental life not because of what you get out of it but for love of God. It is a first step in eradicating self-love from your relationship with God.

Darkness can also be intellectual. This will often manifest itself as doubts. You will sit in Mass and although you do believe - for if you attempted to renounce God and the Faith you would struggle to do so - you are plagued by doubts of the intellect. Is the Blessed Sacrament really God? Goes God really exist? Does heaven really exist? And so on.

Do not be afraid when this happens. It does not mean that you have lost your faith or fallen from a state of grace. The soul experiencing this type of trial knows God but for a time God hides himself from the intellect.

Sometimes the soul can also feel abandoned by God. In such cases, the soul no longer has any sense of God being present or supporting it. The soul feels alone and very far from God. The reality, however, is that while the soul does not perceive God, it is in fact very close to God - or rather

God is very close to the soul. God is drawing the soul near to him while remaining hidden from it.[35]

These trials might occur for very short periods of time, interspersed with consolations and quiet contemplation. For some it will last for weeks, months or even years at a time. Ask God for perseverance during these times. A good spiritual director is vital.

There is one more facet of prayer that I need to discuss with you and that is composure and distraction.

Early on, the intellect and imagination can be very active when one tries to pray. Sometimes their activity makes it hard to remain focused on God.

It is somewhat similar to when you must interrupt a task to run after a toddler and pre-schooler when they are misbehaving. The mere effort to get them to behave and quiet down makes you lose focus on whatever it was that you were initially working on or attempting to do.

Later on this problem can subside and the soul is quiet - it experiences an interior peace and calm. Here God holds the will, intellect, emotions and imagination. The soul is in and with God, and the emotions, intellect and imagination are still. They do not fight God's embrace but happily cease their busy activity for a period to behold him. The soul is calmly aware of God and rests in him.

Following this are further stages of spiritual union. I have insufficient experience and understanding to say anything of use on the topic. Read the *Interior Castle* by St Teresa of Avila for further instruction. The treatise, *Heaven in Faith* by Blessed Elizabeth of the Trinity is also insightful.

Some words of caution: no consolations[36] or periods of darkness should be sought out or desired by you. They are to be given by God to the soul when and as he sees fit. To seek them out or request them puts the soul in peril. Do not presume that you can handle any of these stages. You should also be aware that spiritual experiences can also come from hell, and it isn't always easy to discern the difference.

Reading List

*Handbook of Prayers*, Scepter Press

St Teresa of Avila, *Life*

St Teresa of Avila, *Interior Castle*

Father Gabriel of St Mary Magdalen, *Divine Intimacy*

# THE MECHANICS

Dear Marie Therese,

I have tried to explain the work of prayer to you and to provide an overview of the preliminary stages of the spiritual life.

This work can be divided into the following:

- prayer;
- participation in the sacraments;
- silence;
- annual retreat;
- fulfilment of duties of state of life;
- obedience;
- study; and
- service.

## Prayer

In the same way that you have a study schedule or daily rota of activities and chores, you should also have a regular schedule of spiritual activities and prayer.

The idea is to bookend your day with morning and evening prayer, and intersperse other prayers throughout your day so that it becomes a continuous period of prayer, sacrifice and adoration. Now I don't mean that you spend your entire day doing vocal prayer and adoration. You must still perform your other duties of life![37] Rather the set periods of prayer allow your heart to remain with God as you do your lay work so that this work is transformed into physical prayer offered to God.

The schedule I suggest is to be worked up to gradually. It is better to start slowly and to steadily build a fortress upon a solid and secure foundation than to quickly erect a tall but vulnerable tower made of flimsy materials.

1. **Start**: wake up at a set time every morning. When you hear the alarm, begin your day by reminding yourself what it is for: *For the glory of God and my eternal salvation!*

2. **Morning Exercises**: read the chapter on Morning Exercises in *Introduction to the Devout Life* by St Francis de Sales.. Start with acts of faith, hope and love. This might include kneeling and saying something like: *Jesus, I believe in you. Jesus, I hope in you. Jesus, I love you.*

   Thank God for having preserved you through the night, and ask pardon for any sins you committed during that time. Include here your daily offering and special intentions. Ask for the graces you need to overcome known and unknown faults. You might then recite three Hail Mary prayers for purity and the St Michael prayer for protection.

3.  **Morning Prayer:** give additional time (fifteen to thirty minutes) to more substantial prayer each morning. You might choose to do this directly after your morning exercises. For you this might mean saying the Divine Office (the Psalter of the Liturgy of the Hours), which will take you through the psalms and prepare you well for religious life (all religious must partake in the Divine Office). Others might choose to read a section from the Bible and meditate on it.

4.  **Daily Mass:** make it a priority to attend daily Mass. Ask God at Mass for the understanding and graces you need to grow in holiness. Remember to spend time in prayer after Mass to thank God for the sacrifice of the Mass.

5.  **Angelus:** discretely stop at noon, if you can, to say the Angelus.

6.  **Study:** assign perhaps ten to fifteen minutes minutes each day to study. You might choose to read the New Testament or a spiritual book.

7.  **Rosary and Divine Mercy Chaplet:** try to say the rosary and chaplet every day. I used to do this on my bus rides to and from university. Now I do it on my afternoon walk with the children.

8. **Blessed Sacrament visit**: do you have the opportunity to duck into a church to adore Our Lord in the tabernacle for a minute or two each day?

9. **Evening Prayer**: you should allot another fifteen to thirty minutes to substantial evening prayer. You might wish to say the evening prayers of the Divine Office or incorporate some spiritual reading and reflection into your routine here.

10. **Evening Exercises**: before you go to bed make an act of faith, hope and love. Examine your conscience. I quite like the examination found in *Handbook of Prayers* by Scepter Publishers. Recite the "Act of Contrition"[38] and pray for protection throughout the night.

This is called a "Plan of Life". There is no formula for how to pray or how to plan your daily prayer routine.[39] What I list above are just suggestions. Please do not think that the path to sanctity consists in fulfilling a list of activities. Rather, what I want to impart to you is this: the key is to have some sort of prayer routine (with time allotted to mental prayer) that you are faithful to in order to develop and practise fidelity to God, so that - in turn - God can teach your soul how to be with and remain in him.

## Participation in the Sacraments

Regular confession and Mass will provide you with many graces. They will help you move beyond voluntary venial sins and start to do battle with your more insidious faults.

In addition to attending Sunday Mass you should also strive to attend daily Mass. Start by attending weekday Mass two or three times a week, and build up from there.

Strive to make a weekly confession of your sins.

### Silence

When God called Samuel, he was asleep. All was quiet. Samuel was in a state of quiet repose. After seeking counsel from Eli (his spiritual director) on what to do, Samuel finally answers - surrounded by silence - "Lord, I am listening".[40] Aspire to be like Samuel. Surround yourself as much as possible with silence and stillness as Samuel did.

One cannot be ready; one cannot answer that she is listening for the Lord without silence. In the words of St Josemaria Escriva, "[s]ilence is the doorkeeper of the interior life."[41]

What do I mean by silence? Silence is both internal and external.

The external imposition of silence is easier than the internal and, in fact, aids it, so I will deal with that first.

Try as much as you can to keep the noise around you to a minimum. When you are in the car, for example, choose classical or sacred music over pop music. If you are already sufficiently detached from pop music or the need to listen to music, then opt for no radio or music while driving. Use the silence of the drive to internally converse with God or sit with him in quiet repose.

The same goes for television and movies. Over time you should try to wean yourself from viewing secular television shows and movies. Set aside, perhaps, one night a month for a movie that is artistically beautiful and modest, or that in some way commemorates the sacred. Informative and edifying documentaries can make for excellent viewing.

People waste much time on the internet and electronic devices. If you can, restrict your access to the computer, email and social media. View only the websites that you must as a student, or those that assist you in fulfilling your duties of state. Anything that takes up too much time or leaves you feeling anxious or agitated should be avoided. If you have trouble restricting your social media use, then delete your accounts. If you spend too much time on the internet then install a program that cuts off your access at certain times of the day or night.

Internal silence is more complicated and not so easily obtained. Internal silence means restraint in one's thought, imagination and emotions so that one can be attuned to the movements of God in one's soul. It is God himself who teaches and brings interior silence to a soul, but the soul must be open to being taught. It must routinely sit with God in prayer (daily prayer, regular Eucharistic Adoration etc.).

## Mortification

St Paul introduces us to the idea of mortification in *Romans 8:13*:

> If you live a life of nature, you are marked out for death; if you *mortify* the ways of nature through the power of the Spirit, you will have life.[42]

Mortification is the voluntary "subjection and denial of bodily passions and appetites by abstinence or self-inflicted pain or discomfort"[43] so as to conform and subordinate them to "the rule of reason and faith, as discerned by the mind."[44]

Although mortification might appear to be something negative, its end is entirely positive. Denying oneself certain indulgences or enforcing certain restrictions is intended to strengthen the will. It will help you develop a habit of sacrifice and self-discipline so that you can grow in virtue. This will aid you in overcoming self-love and self-preference so that you can consistently love others through the free gift of yourself.

One way to think about mortification is to have in mind an athlete. An athlete trains regularly and imposes repetitious physical exercises over and over again to strengthen his body and will. All this is done so that the athlete's performance at a meet or competition is improved. In other words, we must train and strengthen our will so that when it really counts, we can be generous; we can exercise self-restraint; we can choose virtue over vice; we can serve rather than be served; we can be kind rather than unkind; we can forsake ourselves for the good of others. Mortification "does not destroy but elevates nature".[45]

It is not necessary at the beginning to take on strenuous physical mortifications. Your day will provide you with many opportunities to mortify yourself. Taking on small domestic chores we find distasteful; cheerfully bearing daily frustrations and disappointments; being kind and patient with a disagreeable colleague at school or work. The list is endless!

Be judicious in which practices you adopt. One way of ensuring temperance is to seek the guidance of your confessor as to the mortifications you take on. Try to be obedient to his advice. If you are told not to undertake a strenuous mortification, then don't. You will please God more with your humility.

### Annual Retreat

Make a point of going on retreat at least once a year. Spiritual retreats give us a beautiful opportunity to connect with Our Lord, to seek solace from the agitations of modern life, and to take stock of where we are and where we should be in our spiritual lives.[46] They are a very important part of the discernment process, and essential to eking out our sanctity in this busy world of ours.

### Fulfilment of Duties of State

What are your "duties of state"? One's "duties of state" are the ordinary obligations and duties associated with one's primary state in life - as a parent, child, student, spouse, priest, religious, etc. Every Catholic must pray and attend Sunday Mass, for example, but we each have an additional set of obligations based on our current position and role. Fulfilling our duties of state with love and perseverance will help us become saints.

### Study

You should know the Sacred Scriptures. Read God's Word. You cannot properly love him if you do not know him. Start with the Gospels. Allocate some time each day to reading a chapter and within a year, you'll have read the entire New Testament.[47] You should also know the teachings of our faith. A good place to start is the *Catechism*. You might also study the writings of the early Church Fathers and St Thomas Aquinas.

You should also learn about the spiritual life. Draw up a reading list and work your way through this list. Read the works of St Teresa of Avila, and St Thérèse of Lisieux. Also read the writings of St Francis de Sales and St Alphonus Liguori.

If you are interested in a particular order, then spend some time learning about that order. Read their rule. Read the writings or biography of their founder, and other important saints within the order.

If Latin, Greek or Hebrew are on offer at your college, consider studying these as part of your undergraduate degree. If you think you might be called to a missionary order, then select a modern language or two as part of your course work.

In addition to all this, you may wish to receive some basic instruction in singing, especially in Gregorian chant.[48]

The Second Vatican Council recognised the primacy of Gregorian chant in the Church's liturgical life.[49] Sacred chant is not a mere aesthetic adornment to the liturgy and our prayer, but a way of placing the entire self - body, intellect and soul - at the service of the liturgy. Chant is an integral part of our Catholic heritage, and religious orders have been pivotal in its development and preservation. Some communities have made recordings of their liturgical prayer. You can listen to these recordings and, in this way, pray with the sisters as you discern.

### Service

Our love for God must express itself in our love for others. We live out this love in a tangible way whenever we engage in spiritual or corporal works of mercy.

What are the spiritual and corporal works of mercy? "The *works of mercy* are charitable actions by which we come to the aid of our neighbour in his spiritual or bodily necessities."[50] The spiritual works of mercy pertain to the spiritual needs of others while the corporal acts of mercy concern their physical or material needs. "Corporal", of course, comes from the Latin word "corpus", meaning body.

One way to ensure that you regularly engage in spiritual and corporal works of mercy is by committing to a weekly or monthly form of service. Once a month, for example, you might assist at a soup kitchen run by the Missionaries of Charity. Alternatively, once a week you might teach English to immigrants or tutor children in a poor neighbourhood. You could also volunteer at a crisis pregnancy centre or homeless shelter for women and children. Consider teaching catechesis at your local parish.

In choosing a form of service, consider the talents and gifts God has endowed you with. Ask yourself: "How can I - with my particular talents, experience and sensibilities - best be of service to others? What areas of Christian service am I naturally drawn to? What concerns me? What inspires me? What do I enjoy? What am I good at?" This exercise will also aid you in discerning which orders you might be called to.

Reading List

*Learn About the Faith*

Leo J. Trese, *The Faith Explained*

*Catechism of the Catholic Church*

*Sacraments*

Reginald Garrigou-Lagrange OP,
*Three Ages of the Interior Life: Prelude to Eternal Life*
Part 2, Chapter 30 ("Sacramental Confession")
Part 2, Chapter 31 ("Assistance at Mass,
the Source of Sanctification")
Part 2, Chapter 32 ("Holy Communion")
Part 3, Chapter 24
("The Sacrifice of the Mass and Proficients")
Part 3, Chapter 25 ("The Communion of Proficients")

*Prayer*

*Handbook of Prayers*, Scepter Press
Francis de Sales, *Introduction to the Devout Life*
Alphonsus Liguori, *How to Converse With God*
Teresa of Avila, *Life*

*Divine Office*

*Morning and Evening Prayer:
With Night Prayer from the Divine Office* (Collins)

*Chant: CDs*

*Mater Eucharistiae*, Dominican Sisters of Mary,
Mother of the Eucharist

*Voices: Chant from Avignon*,
Benedictine Sisters of Le Barroux

# DATING

Dear Marie Therese,

Under no circumstances should you be dating.

An inability to refrain from dating during discernment is usually a sign that the soul is not called to religious life.

Also, know that dating can induce an emotional attachment to a person (even if the courtship is chaste), which will cloud your ability to freely discern what God is asking of you. A large part of the discernment and preparation process is gradual detachment - from worldly things, from others, from vice and sin, from one's preferences and so on - so that you can respond promptly and immediately to God's call to enter religious life.

Dating will make this very difficult. Dating can also give rise to occasions of sin or worse. You cannot do the job of discerning and preparing for religious life if you have to do constant battle trying to preserve your purity. Falling into sins of impurity can lead not only to the loss of grace (in the case of mortal sin) but also the loss of a vocation.

If you do enter religious life after dating, any imprudent or unchaste actions, discussions or choices you made while dating will remain in your memory and can taint your imagination. The sins of your past will make it harder for you to live out your life as a religious in holiness and with perfection.

Dating during discernment is also selfish and shows a lack of charity for others. When I was a young, single woman, it was not unheard of for men in the "Catholic singles" community to date women while concurrently discerning a vocation to the priesthood.

What a poor way to treat Jesus! What a poor way to treat the women they took out on dates! A person who dates while discerning shows a lack of prudence and charity towards others, obliviousness to scandal and a dearth of resilience. Let this not be you!

# MODESTY

Dear Marie Therese,

As you enter into serious discernment and preparation for religious life, you should develop some detachment about your dress and appearance. You already dress quite modestly. Continue to do so. Ask God to help you grow in this area - not just in dress but in speech and attitude too.[51]

Do not place too much importance on your appearance. Develop a love for the simple. Try to be frugal. Make do with what you have, and when you do need to acquire new clothes or shoes, favour quality and practicality over style. Avoid the ostentatious, and restrict yourself in terms of spending.

Take care to dress well for Jesus when you attend Mass. As a rule, tight or revealing clothing is a bad idea. Just as it is an act of charity to others to dress neatly, it is also an act of charity to dress in a way that doesn't attract too much or the wrong kind of attention to yourself while in discernment.[52]

One day St Francis de Sales saw St Jane Frances de Chantal better dressed than usual. She was then a young widow and had not yet entered religious life. St Francis de Sales asked her, "Madam, do you wish to marry again?" When she replied, "no", he said, "Very well but then you should pull down your flag."[53]

You'll find all this easier to do if you have a healthy understanding of your beauty and worth. Consider what it is that makes you beautiful to God. Remember always that God loves you! He died on the cross for you. You are a precious daughter of Christ and it is in this that you are most beautiful:

> Down deep we all know that clothing and jewellery are not the person. The individual in elegant evening dress is not one atom different from the same person in paint-smeared work clothes. The Christian is immeasurably more interested in the splendour of truth, the symphony of music, the beauty of nature and art, the glory of prayer and selfless human love. These are values no thief can reach, no moth destroy (*Lk* 12:33).[54]

Ask Our Lady to tutor you in modesty. Dress for God and for God alone.

# THE LITTLE WAY
## OF THE SINNER:
### OFFERING GOD OUR FAILURES

Dear Marie Therese,

God loves all of you and he wants all of you. This means that - whether you are called to religious life or not - he desires that you offer him both your best and your worst. He cannot transform you in love until you give *everything* to him.

We tend to want to offer God only what is good. But we must realise that we should give him our faults and failures too. We can make offerings even of these!

If you feel discouraged by the fact you were distracted during Mass, then offer up both the distraction and your discouragement to him. If you spoke poorly of another, offer the detraction as well as the disappointment you feel in yourself to him.

If St Thérèse's spirituality was "the little way" then this can be thought of as the *little way of the sinner*. You will make great strides in humility by doing this. You will also find great peace.[55]

The spiritual life can be difficult and it is easy to fall into pride (when we fail to realise how little or imperfect we are) or despair (when we consider sanctity to be an impossible task because we do not see yet that it is God who perfects us). Pride and despair are similar in that they eradicate joy. The proud person is self-satisfied but does not possess a joy that is selfless or readily shared with others. The person in despair is miserable, and as self-focused and joyless as the proud.

What a relief it is to realise that our sanctity doesn't depend on our perfection - but on God's perfection in us. And that God cannot perfect us until we hand him all our sins, failures and faults - the bad as well as the good. God can transform us through our sins and faults provided we go to him in humility. Our weaknesses and imperfections are all we really have that are truly our own.

This should give us great hope! To know that all we have to do is go to him with our messes and scrapes. That we need only lay them at his feet like a child, tell him "I am sorry", and then ask for his help. He is our loving Father and he will not deny us.

# THE MAGDALENE:

## HEALING AND CONVERSION

Dear Marie Therese,

Not every young woman called to religious life has been as well catechised or blessed with the loving and stable family life you have.

Some of us were raised in Catholic families but were poorly formed. We didn't receive the spiritual or intellectual formation we needed, and so we don't know our faith the way we should. Some women come to religious life as converts. They have lived in the world, according to the ways of the world, and then found Our Lord and entered into friendship with him.

Others don't have a life changing conversion but as cradle or "rocking horse" Catholics[56] must engage in a life-long battle against lukewarmness and mediocrity.

Many have also been hurt by divorce, neglect, or abuse. They carry emotional and spiritual scars associated with the widespread breakdown of the family and the sexual revolution. These wounds can lead to a lack of inner freedom - they stop us from loving others and ourselves in ways that are wholesome and free. They stop us from seeing ourselves as we really are - beautiful, beloved daughters of God.

None of these wounds, however, will stop God from calling a woman to religious life if it is his will. God does not restrict himself to human expectations or measures of respectability.

St Mary Magdalene, or the Magdalene as she is sometimes known, had seven demons cast out of her. She is traditionally thought to have been a prostitute. She met Our Lord and became one of the greatest saints in the history of the Church. It was she rather than the Apostles to whom Our Lord first appeared after his Resurrection.[57]

St Margaret of Cortona was a rich man's "mistress" and had a child out of wedlock. She entered religious life and died a saint.[58]

St Josephine Bakhita was born in Sudan and abducted from her parents by Arab slave traders at only eight or so years of age.[59] She was made a slave, forced to convert to Islam and then sold and bought many times over. Some of her owners were cruel and physically abused her.[60] One mutilated her skin with a razor and salt causing over a hundred scars on her torso and right arm.[61] St Josephine Bakhita eventually became a Canossian religious sister and one of the great saints of modern Africa.

Ignorance, degradation, and trauma - none of these will hold Our Lord back from calling a woman to be a saint or religious sister if he so desires. There is simply no accounting for grace.

Women who come to religious life with a more difficult or unconventional background will, however, have some hurdles to overcome.

I am told that one of the biggest problems faced by candidates for religious life is a lack of knowledge about the Catholic faith. A priest wrote to say:

> In my pastoral experience, a basic catechesis is lacking in young Catholic people. Most seminaries and religious houses offer basic catechetics to incoming candidates for it simply is not there. There may be a love of the Lord and a recent conversion, but an understanding of virtue, grace, human nature, the teachings of the Church, are not there.

This is easily corrected with some diligence. I encourage you to buy a copy of Leo Trese's introduction to the Catholic faith called *The Faith Explained*. It provides an excellent overview of our beautiful faith.

A second hurdle concerns the emotional and spiritual wounds inflicted by divorce and the sexual revolution. If this applies to you, begin to heal your wounds before you enter religious life. This is the more difficult task and it will require prayer, humility and perseverance.

## Spiritual Healing

Start by entrusting the healing process to St Mary Magdalene. Ask the Magdalene to be your special patroness as you address the instability and wounds you received during your upbringing or as a young adult in the secular world.

Ask God to show you what wounds you have. Ask him to heal them. Ask him to give you the grace to co-operate with his healing.

Receive the Sacrament of Penance and Reconciliation. This is God's preferred method of healing and it is a most precious gift. Go to confession on a weekly or fortnightly basis, and you'll receive much grace to overcome your spiritual wounds, venial sins and involuntary faults.

Women who have struggled with impurity (however bad) and who are called to religious life should pray for perseverance in holy purity but also for a healing of their emotions and imagination. Conversely, women who have lived chastely need to be wary of spiritual pride. This sort of pride is extremely poisonous. Ask God for humility.

Women who have been abused or neglected should pray that God take away the distorted and muddied filters through which they see themselves so that they can appreciate their true worth - their infinite value as a child of God. Healing won't happen overnight but with grace and persistent effort, you will become the woman God has always intended you to be.

Emotional Healing

Catholics sometimes resist or belittle therapy. We forget that we are physical and emotional beings as well as spiritual beings. We hope that prayer and the sacraments will suffice. Sometimes they do but God also wants us to benefit from the wisdom and gifts of our fellow Christians and for this reason, seeing a Catholic therapist can be extremely helpful.

Do seek out therapy if there have been difficulties in your life that need attention, discussion and healing. However, please remember this important proviso: make sure your therapist is a committed Catholic!

While some Catholics refuse to see therapy as a useful tool, others jump right in and are undiscerning about the advice they are given or the therapist they see. Some therapists, psychologists or psychiatrists do not understand our Catholic faith. At best they see it as a dispensable. At worst they view it with hostility and suspicion, and will try to "release" you from the "burden" of your Judeo-Christian beliefs. These therapists do great harm to the Christians and Catholics who stumble into their counsel.

Reading List

*Conversions*

Mother Veronica Namoyo Le Goulard PCC,
*A Memory for Wonders: A True Story*

Caryll Houselander, *A Rocking Horse Catholic*

Evelyn Waugh, *Brideshead Revisited* (fiction)

Graham Greene, *The End of the Affair* (fiction)

*Faith Formation*

Leo J. Trese, *The Faith Explained*

# Some Practical Matters

Dear Marie Therese,

I would like to address some issues that will arise as you discern and prepare for religious life.

## Debt

One requirement for entry into religious life is that the candidate be debt free. You have done well to avoid debt at university. Continue to be frugal and self-disciplined in how you spend your money. Live within your means and - whatever you do - do not go into debt.[62]

## Investigate

Take time to investigate and learn about religious life. Right now your knowledge is mostly theoretical. You need to understand the basic differences between the enclosed and semi-active orders, and you should start to develop a sense for the different charisms of the various orders open to you.

What is a charism? The charism of a religious order is the particular way in which its members are called to love and serve God. It is given by God to the order as a gift for the benefit of the entire Church, and is what gives the order its particular character or orientation.[63]

The Dominicans are called, for example, to contemplate God and to give to others the fruits of their contemplation. It is for this reason that they are known as the Order of Preachers. The Franciscans are called to live out the Gospel of Our Lord Jesus Christ in a particular way and to proclaim the Gospel to others.

To begin your understanding of religious life, start by reading a delightful book entitled, *A Few Lines to Tell You: My Life in Carmel* by Sister Marie OCD It is difficult to find but well worth the expense and effort of obtaining a second-hand copy. More readily available is the book, *A Right to Be Merry* by Mother Mary Francis PCC, which describes life in a Poor Clare cloister. *Barefoot Journey* by Sister Felicity PCC is also about the Poor Clares.

*In This House of Brede* by Rumer Godden should be available through your library system, and provides a delightful, fictional account of life in an enclosed, Benedictine priory. The first few chapters of *The Deliverance of Sister Cecilia* by William Brinkley describe the life of a sister upon entering a semi-active religious order. This book is an easy, edifying read.

My advice to you - and I cannot press this upon you enough - is to spend a week with a contemplative order and a week with a semi-active order as soon as you can.

Ask St Faustina to intercede for you in finding the right order. After she entered the Sisters of Our Lady of Mercy, she decided to leave so she could enter an enclosed, contemplative order. She wanted more time to devote to prayer than what was possible with the Sisters of Our Lady of Mercy (a semi-active community). Our Lord appeared to her with open wounds on his face and crying large tears. He rebuked her for this decision saying:

> It is you who will cause Me this pain if you leave this convent. It is to this place that I called you and nowhere else; and I have prepared many graces for you.[64]

### Some Additional Considerations

When considering which religious order to join, look for orders that are vibrant, joyful and which strive to be faithful, not only to the Church and its traditions and teachings, but also the rule and traditions of their own order and founder. Attempting to join an order in decline with the intention of reform is likely to lead to frustration and a possible loss of vocation.

Some women might toy with the idea of starting a new order. Try to keep in mind that very few souls are called to found orders and many of them receive this calling only after they have entered religious life.[65] God will make it clear if you are called to begin something new. Until he does, assume that you are not and that you need to find an established order to join.

## Impediments

Certain physical, mental or emotional disabilities will prevent you from entering religious life.

To enter a particular order, you need to be capable of doing all that is demanded of the sisters in that order. If you have a physical, mental or emotional handicap that will prevent you from fulfilling your duties of state, then you probably don't have a vocation to that order - if at all.

One of the most common impediments I have seen in young women desiring the religious life is depression. If you have or are struggling with clinical depression, you will likely be refused entry. The same goes for bipolar disorder, schizophrenia, and all the various personality disorders.

If you find yourself in this position, do not be ashamed or feel humiliated. It is hard not to feel rejected, but ask God for the grace to love your cross.

Caryll Houselander, a "divine eccentric" who lived in England during the last century, struggled with what she termed "neurosis" but argued - I believe correctly - that "neurosis" or mental and emotional difficulties can be a means of achieving great sanctity. This particular cross, with all its sorrow, mental anguish, lack of emotional control, humiliation, judgement, and exclusion, can be a path to sanctity when united to Jesus's suffering on the cross and in the Garden of Gethsemane. You might not become a religious sister, but you can still become a saint.

## Exceptions

There are, of course, exceptions to some impediments. Sometimes an order - because of its charism - can accept women with particular needs.

There is an order in France, the Institute of the Little Sisters Disciples of the Lamb, where young women with Down's syndrome can enter religious life. Also of French origin are the Dominican Sisters of Bethany, who work with incarcerated women and sometimes welcome formerly imprisoned women into their order as religious sisters. The Order of the Visitation of the Virgin Mary was founded by St Francis de Sales and St Jane Frances de Chantal "as a haven for those whose health, age or other considerations debarred them from the already established orders."[66]

## Pilgrimages and Mission Trips

There is a popular maxim in the spiritual life that God is never outdone in generosity.[67] It is not uncommon, therefore, to hear that a particular priest discovered his vocation while attending World Youth Day or that a young woman was confirmed in her decision to enter religious life after a pilgrimage to Rome, the Holy Land or a Marian shrine.

If you are having trouble discerning or feel trepidation about entering religious life, consider going on pilgrimage to a shrine of Our Lady or some other holy place to ask Mary and the saints to intercede on your behalf.

You don't need to travel far to make a pilgrimage. If a longer trip isn't possible, look for shrines and holy places near you, or within easy travel distance. You might also consider setting aside a few months, or perhaps even a year, to do mission work: serving the needs of others by engaging in spiritual and/or corporal works of mercy.

Reading List

*Debt Avoidance*

Dave Ramsey, *The Total Money Makeover:
A Proven Plan for Financial Fitness*

*Investigate*

Sister Marie OCD,
*A Few Lines to Tell You: My Life in Carmel*

Mother Mary Francis PCC, *A Right to Be Merry*

Sister Felicity PCC, *Barefoot Journey*

Rumer Godden, *In This House of Brede* (fiction)

William Brinkley, *The Deliverance of Sister Cecilia* (fiction)

*Impediments*

Abbott William, *A Calling: An Autobiography and the
Founding of the Maronite Monks of Adoration.*

*For Parents*

Brett Brannen, *A Priest in the Family: A Guide for
Parents Whose Sons Are Considering Priesthood*

# QUAGMIRES

Dear Marie Therese,

Unfortunately, it is not uncommon for souls considering religious life to end up in a discernment quagmire. They won't enter religious life but they can't quite abandon the idea that they are called either. Such souls can toy with the idea of religious life for years on end.

This is often because they want a clear and definite "yes" from God before they enter. This is a mistake. Rather, what you should be looking for is a clear and definite "no". Ask yourself this:

Has God made it clear that he is *not* calling me to religious life?

The modern emphasis on the need for an unequivocal affirmative command from God to enter religious life is misdirected and creates unnecessary suffering. God sometimes does make it very clear to certain souls that they are called. He gives them a definitive "yes". But not everyone has this experience.

If you have started discernment and made progress in the spiritual life but do not yet know with certainty, make your move and enter religious life. Assume that you *are* called and start your postulancy. This is simply the next stage of your discernment. It is the natural next step.

By doing this, you place your vocation into the hands of God's Church. God will use his Church to help you discern.

One of the ways in which your superiors will assess whether you have an authentic vocation to religious life is by observing you throughout the postulancy and novitiate periods to see how you get on. Do you flourish in religious life? What is the fruit?[68]

And so, rather than asking God over and over again, "am I called?", recite this prayer instead:

Dear God, please give me the courage and strength to enter the convent. If religious life is not for me, please make it abundantly clear and prevent me from progressing further.

# Do Not Delay

Dear Marie Therese,

Once you see that you are or might be called to religious life, do not delay in entering.

I was shocked to hear from a priest that he knew of a number of souls who understand they have a vocation but continually put off entering religious life - choosing instead to tend to this or that, complete a masters degree, enrol in a doctorate, take some trip or wait for some milestone to pass, etc.

Marie Therese, we must pray for these souls! They hurt not only themselves but the Church too.

They remind me of couples who know they are to marry but enter into a protracted and extended courtship or engagement lasting many years. They open themselves to all sorts of dangers and occasions of sin. Worst of all, they risk losing their beloved as a spouse.

One must also be careful not to spend too long in discernment. Love of God must be manifest in our choices and actions. It is not enough to want God. We must choose God.

Discerning for years on end, as I did, is more often than not a symptom of self-absorption and an inability to follow good intentions with appropriate actions.

If this is something you are struggling with, implore the help of St Gabriel of the Sorrowful Virgin - a young Passionist saint who died at age twenty-five. St Gabriel put off entering religious life even though he knew he was called by God to be a religious. He wanted to finish university. He wanted to continue a life in which he could read popular novels and attend the dances and social events he so very much enjoyed. He liked expensive, fashionable clothes. He did not want to displease or inconvenience his father. In short, he had a difficult time renouncing his secular dreams and desire for pleasure and success.

St Gabriel fell mortally ill not once but twice, and both times promised that he would enter religious life, only to put it off once he recovered. The young saint was able to break with his old way of life only after a locution from Our Lady. As he gazed one day at a beautiful icon of Our Lady, St Gabriel heard Mary's voice in his soul: "Francis, why do you linger in the world? Arise, make haste, and become a religious."[69]

If you think you might be called then decisively cut your ties to the world and enter. As Our Lady said to St Gabriel: "Arise, make haste, and become a religious!"

Do not delay!

## Endnotes

[1] In the tradition of St Teresa of Avila, St Thérèse of Lisieux, and so on, I use the term "soul" to describe the person and her engagement in the spiritual life. This is not meant to suggest or endorse a dualistic vision of the human person.

[2] St Augustine, St Francis of Assisi, St Francis Xavier etc.

[3] Christ's public life was from age thirty to thirty-three until his death.

[4] Christ fulfilled the duties of state associated with his life as a child and young adult perfectly. See the section "Fulfilment of Duties of State" in the chapter titled "The Mechanics" for more on this topic.

[5] St Maria Faustina Kowalska, *Diary: Divine Mercy in My Soul*, #9-10.

[6] Thomas Edward Bridgett, *Life and Writings of Sir Thomas More: Lord Chancellor of England and Martyr* (1982) Burns & Oates, p. 23.

[7] Something like this: *Dear Jesus, if You do not want me to be a religious, please do not allow me to enter the convent. Allow me to be rejected or deterred in some way. If You do wish me to enter, then please allow and facilitate it.* Also pray for the grace to love your vocation, whatever that might be.

[8] "Diligent discernment" is another term used to describe this type of discernment. Brett A. Brannen, *To Save a Thousand Souls: A Guide for*

*Discerning a Vocation to Diocesan Priesthood* (2013) Vianney Vocations, pp. 157-158.

[9] Brett A. Brannen, *To Save a Thousand Souls: A Guide for Discerning a Vocation to Diocesan Priesthood* (2013) Vianney Vocations, p. 175.

[10] Be aware of the modern tendency to romanticise romantic love. The culture around you is saturated with the idea that we should aspire to be "in love". By choosing religious life you might think that you're missing out. The type of love marketed to you by pop songs, movies, television shows, magazines and even operas, is not the same as married love. Marriage is more like a marathon than a sprint. The early feelings of infatuation do not last. With the grace of God, this immature love should evolve into something more profound – much deeper and much more stable. It is not, however, the same as the initial infatuation common in courtship and early marriage.

[11] Maggio cited in Richard Butler, *Religious Vocations: An Unnecessary Mystery* (1961) Tan, p. 58.

[12] *1 Corinthians 7.*

[13] *Summa Theologica* Pt II-II Q 189 Art 1.

[14] *Summa Theologica* Pt II-II Q 189 Art 10.

[15] Also see *Mark 10:17-31* and *Luke 18:18-30.*

[16] Recognising that religious life is more efficacious than marriage in preparing one for heaven does not necessarily imply that marriage is poor, bad or worthless.

[17] Our marriage is a beautiful gift and blessing to me. First, I have certain wounds and weaknesses that have been greatly healed through my marriage. My husband's love and loyalty to me are a reflection of God's own love and faithfulness, and I have flourished within the loving, protective confines of this relational tabernacle. Second, our "calling" to be adoptive parents is a most beautiful gift. God has entrusted our children to us and I am delighted to be the mother of these precious little souls.

[18] Emphasis added.

[19] This, of course, does not conflict with the universal call to holiness which was also proclaimed by the Council in *Lumen Gentium*. See the chapter of this book titled "A Universal Call to Sanctity".

[20] Emphasis as in original text. John Paul II, *Vita Consecrata #32*.

[21] Agnes Newton Keith, *Three Came Home* (1947) Little, Brown and Company, p. 100.

[22] Ibid, pp. 100-101. Emphasis as in original.

[23] Ibid, p. 104.

[24] Edith Stein, "The Separate Vocations of Man and Woman According to Nature and Grace" in *The Collected Works of Edith Stein, Volume 2: Essays on Woman*, Second edition (ICS Publications), p. 59. Emphasis as in original.

[25] Ibid.

[26] Gertrude von Le Fort, *The Song at the Scaffold* (2011) Ignatius Press, p. 57.

[27] Typically corporal or spiritual works of mercy.

[28] This is not to say, however, that you shouldn't also seek out the advice and guidance of a religious sister as you discern.

[29] St Teresa of Avila, *Life*, Chapter XIII #24-29.

[30] The restraint cautioned by a director can be as important as the encouragement he gives.

[31] A scruple is an "unfounded apprehension and consequently unwarranted fear that something is a sin which, as a matter of fact, is not. It is not considered here so much as an isolated act, but rather as an habitual state of mind known to directors of souls as a 'scrupulous conscience.' St Alphonsus describes it as a condition in which one influenced by trifling reasons, and without any solid foundation, is often afraid that sin lies where it really does not. ... The judgement is seriously warped, the moral power tired out in futile combat, and then not unfrequently the scrupulous person makes shipwreck of salvation either on the Scylla of despair or the Charybdis of unheeding indulgence

in vice." Joseph Delany, 'Scruple', *Catholic Encyclopedia* (1912).

[32] *Introduction to the Devout Life*: Part I, Chapter 4: "The Pursuit of the Devout Life Requires a Guide", and Part II, Chapter 19: "Of Holy Confession".

[33] Ibid.

[34] St Thérèse of Lisieux, *Story of A Soul* (1976, translated by John Clarke, OCD), ICS Publications, 242-243.

[35] Only in retrospect is one usually able to see what God was doing and how God was supporting the soul at the time.

[36] This includes emotional consolations, locutions, intellectual lights, prayer of the quiet, spiritual union or signs.

[37] Our duties of state include prayer. Our duties are both horizontal (owed to our fellow man) and vertical (owed to God). See the subheading titled "Fulfillment of Duties of State" in this chapter.

[38] Act of Contrition: *Oh my God, I am heartily sorry for having offended you, and I detest all my sins, because I dread the loss of heaven and the pains of hell; but most of all because they offend you, my God, who are all good and deserving of my love I firmly resolve, with the help of your grace, to sin no more and avoid all occasions of sin.* See also *Handbook of Prayers*, Scepter Press, p. 62.

[39] For other examples see Elisabeth Leseur's "Plan of Life" in *The Secret Diary of Elisabeth Leseur: The Woman Whose Goodness Changed her Husband from Atheist to Priest* (2002) Sophia Institute Press, pp. 68-74. The "Rule of Life" adopted by St Teresa of the Andes prior to her entry into religious life can be found in letters #30, #35 (duties of state), #36 (prayer, spiritual union and spiritual reading), #45 (prayer, duties of state and sacrifice), published in *Letters of St Teresa of the Andes* (1994, translated by Michael D. Griffin OCD) Teresian Charism Press. A more concise summary of Teresa's "Rule of Life" is provided by Jennifer Moorcroft in *God is All Joy: The Life of St Teresa of the Andes*, (2009) ICS Publications, pp. 69-70.

[40] *1 Samuel 3*.

[41] St Josemaria Escriva, *The Way* #281.

[42] Emphasis added. The translation I use here is from the Knox Bible. The translation from the Navarre Bible, which I rely on elsewhere is as follows: "for if you live according to the flesh you will die, but if by the Spirit you put to death the deeds of the body you will live." See also *Colossians 3:5* and *Galatians 5:24*.

[43] *Merriam-Webster*.

[44] 'Mortification' (1911) *The Catholic Encyclopedia*.

[45] Ibid.

[46] Ibid.

[47] Make sure the Bible you read is an approved translation. Have your confessor check that the version you select is unproblematic. It is also prudent to be reading an approved commentary at the same time.

[48] It is possible to chant the psalms, which make up the Divine Office, and to chant the Ordo of Holy Mass. Likewise, many beautiful hymns of the Church's sacred music tradition have been translated into the vernacular with their original melodies - Adoro Te Devote; Stabat Mater; O Salutaris Hostia; Te Deum.

[49] *Sacrosanctum Concilium* #116.

[50] *Catechism of the Catholic Church* 2447.

[51] Modesty starts with our dress but we should also strive to be modest in our words, postures, actions and thoughts.

[52] You might choose, for example, not to wear make up, color your hair or paint your nails as you prepare to enter religious life.

[53] *Butler's Lives of the Saints* 3, p. 370.

[54] Thomas Dubay, *Happy Are You Poor: The Simple Life and Spiritual Freedom* (1981) Ignatius Press, pp. 121-122.

[55] Note that this "way" is not to be used as a justification or excuse for sin. It is, rather, a way of allowing God to use our inevitable falls and failings as a means of drawing us closer to Him.

[56] This is how the late mystic, Caryll Houselander described herself in her autobiography, *A Rocking Horse Catholic*.

[57] *Butler's Lives of the Saints* 3, pp. 161-163.

[58] *Butler's Lives of the Saints* 1, pp. 396-399.

[59] Roberto Italo Zanini, *Bakhita: From Slave to Saint* (2013) Ignatius, p. 37.

[60] Ibid, pp. 56-57.

[61] Ibid, pp. 59-61.

[62] This includes credit card debt.

[63] See *1 Corinthians 12:7* and *1 Peter 4:10*.

[64] St Maria Faustina Kowalska, *Diary: Divine Mercy in My Soul*, #19.

[65] The most recent saintly example being Mother Teresa. She was called to found the Missionaries of Charity only after she was a Loreto sister.

[66] *Butler's Lives of the Saints* 3, p. 371.

[67] See *2 Corinthians 9:6-15*.

[68] Brett Brannen, *A Priest in the Family: A Guide for Parents Whose Sons are Considering Priesthood* (2014) Vianney Vocations, p. 36.

[69] Camillus Barth, *Boy in a Hurry: The Story of St. Gabriel of the Sorrowful Virgin* (1987) the ECO Press, p. 21.